HAL•LEONARD®
PIANO PLAY-ALONG

PIANO | VOCAL | GUITAR • AUDIO

VOLUME 20

AUDIO
ACCESS
INCLUDED

LA LA LAND

MUSIC FROM THE MOTION PICTURE SOUNDTRACK

Audio Arrangements by Peter Deneff

PLAYBACK+
Speed • Pitch • Balance • Loop

D1229217

ISBN 978-1-4950-9985-4

HAL•LEONARD®
7777 W. BLUEMOUND RD. P.O. BOX 13819 MILWAUKEE, WI 53213

In Australia Contact:
Hal Leonard Australia Pty. Ltd.
4 Lentara Court
Cheltenham, Victoria, 3192 Australia
Email: ausadmin@halleonard.com.au

Visit Hal Leonard Online at
www.halleonard.com

ANOTHER DAY OF SUN

Music by JUSTIN HURWITZ
Lyrics by BENJ PASEK
& JUSTIN PAUL

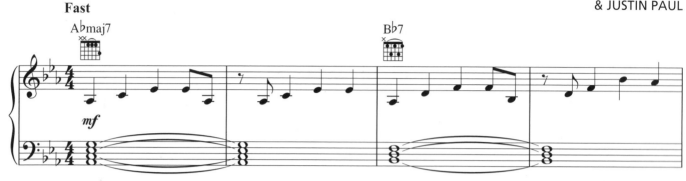

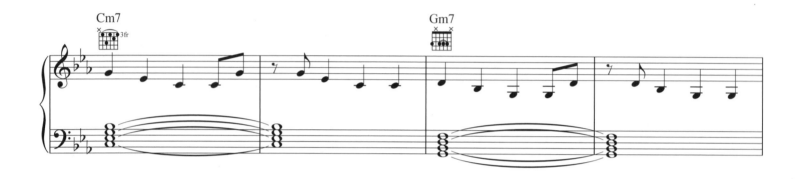

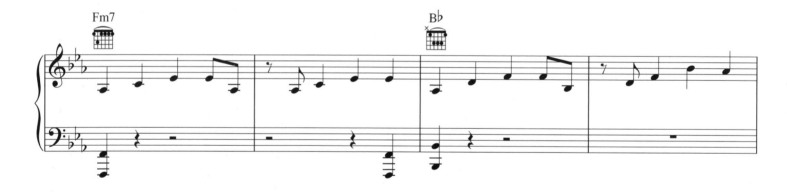

11

CITY OF STARS

Music by JUSTIN HURWITZ
Lyrics by BENJ PASEK
& JUSTIN PAUL

Sebastian: City of stars, _ are you shining just for me?

City of stars, _ there's so much that I can't see.

Who

AUDITION
(The Fools Who Dream)

Music by JUSTIN HURWITZ
Lyrics by BENJ PASEK
& JUSTIN PAUL

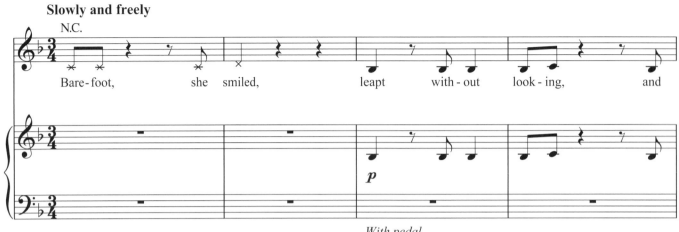

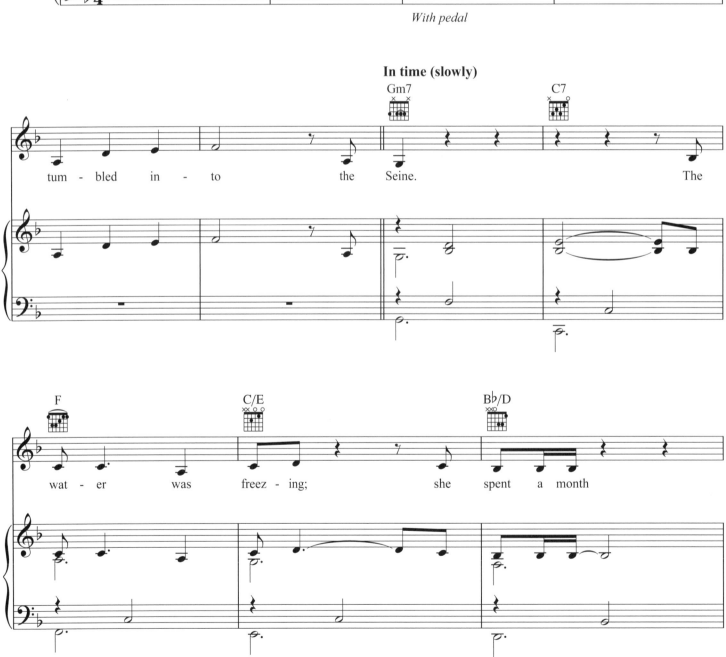

A LOVELY NIGHT

Music by JUSTIN HURWITZ
Lyrics by BENJ PASEK
& JUSTIN PAUL

Fm7 | Bb7 | Ebmaj7 | Bb9

not a spark in sight. __ What a waste of a love-ly night. __

Eb | Am7 | D13 | G+

A bit faster

Mia: You say there's noth-ing here; well

poco accel.

Adim | B7 | Em7 | D7 | Gmaj7 | G+

let's make some-thing clear: I think I'll be the one __ to make that __ call. And though you look so cute in your

Sebastian (spoken): But you'll call.

Adim | B7 | Em7 | D7 | Gmaj7

pol-y-es-ter suit, you're right: I'd nev-er fall for you at all. And

It's wool.

MIA & SEBASTIAN'S THEME

Music by
JUSTIN HURWITZ

PLANETARIUM

Music by
JUSTIN HURWITZ

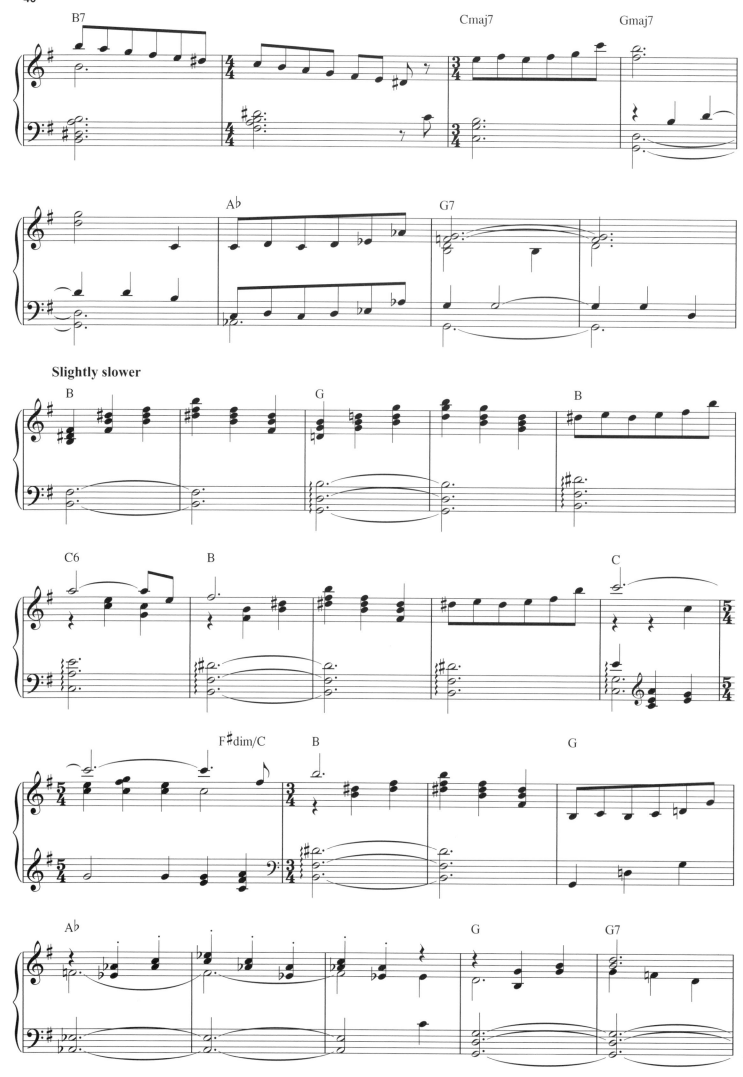

SOMEONE IN THE CROWD

Music by JUSTIN HURWITZ
Lyrics by BENJ PASEK
& JUSTIN PAUL

Bright Broadway two-beat feel

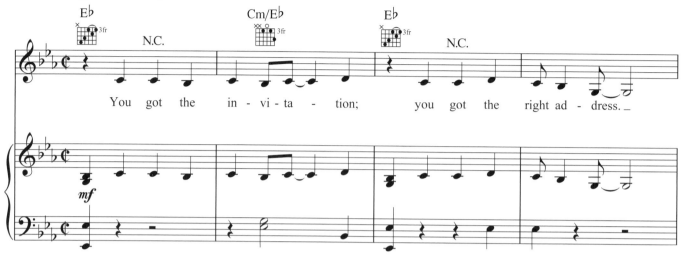

You got the in-vi-ta-tion; you got the right ad-dress.

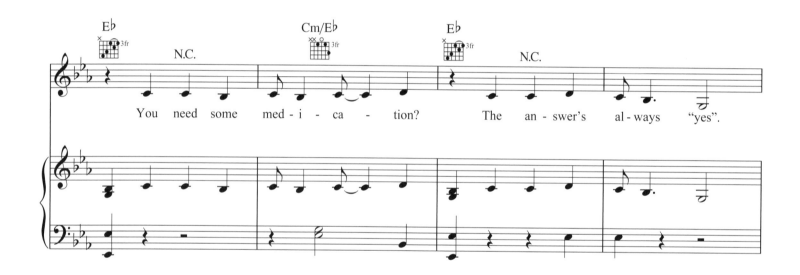

You need some med-i-ca-tion? The an-swer's al-ways "yes".

A lit-tle chance en-coun-ter could be the one you've wait-

stay be - hind. (You've got to go and ___ find...) _____

(Spoken): that some - one in ___ the crowd. ___

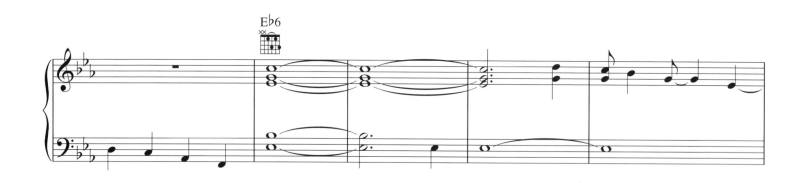

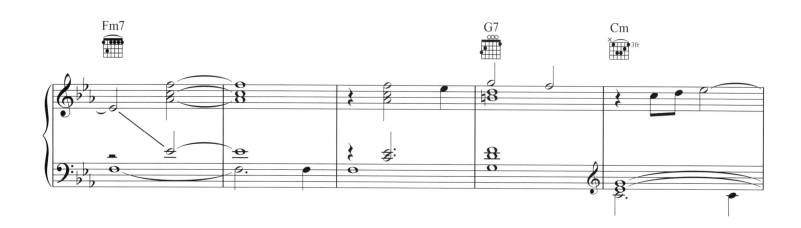

52

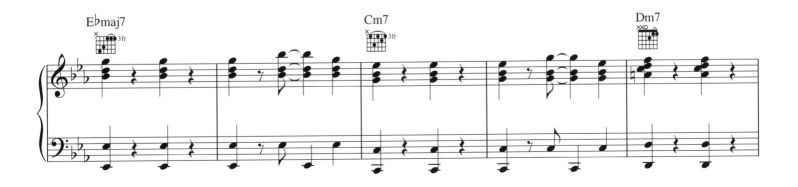

START A FIRE

Music & Lyrics by JOHN STEPHENS,
ANGÉLIQUE CINÉLU, MARIUS DE VRIES
and JUSTIN HURWITZ

(We can start _ a fi -
Solo ends

D.S. al Coda

don't you know, _   don't you know, _____   to - night. _

THE ULTIMATE SONGBOOKS

Hal•Leonard®
PIANO PLAY-ALONG

AUDIO ACCESS INCLUDED

These great songbooks come with our standard arrangements for piano and voice with guitar chord frames plus audio.

Each book includes either a CD or access to online recordings of full performance of each song, as well as a second track without the piano part so you can play "lead" with the band!

1. MOVIE MUSIC
00311072 P/V/G $14.95

5. DISNEY
00311076 P/V/G $14.99

7. LOVE SONGS
00311078 P/V/G $14.95

8. THE PIANO GUYS – UNCHARTED
00202549 P/V/G $24.99

10. WEDDING CLASSICS
00311081 Piano Solo $14.95

12. CHRISTMAS FAVORITES
00311137 P/V/G $15.95

13. YULETIDE FAVORITES
00311138 P/V/G $14.95

14. POP BALLADS
00311145 P/V/G $14.95

15. FAVORITE STANDARDS
00311146 P/V/G $14.95

17. MOVIE FAVORITES
00311148 P/V/G $14.95

19. CONTEMPORARY HITS
00311162 P/V/G $14.95

21. BIG BAND
00311164 P/V/G $14.95

22. ROCK CLASSICS
00311165 P/V/G $14.95

23. WORSHIP CLASSICS
00311166 P/V/G $14.95

24. LES MISÉRABLES
00311169 P/V/G $14.99

25. THE SOUND OF MUSIC
00311175 P/V/G $15.99

28. LENNON & McCARTNEY
00311180 P/V/G $14.95

29. THE BEACH BOYS
00311181 P/V/G $14.95

30. ELTON JOHN
00311182 P/V/G $14.95

31. CARPENTERS
00311183 P/V/G $14.95

32. ADELE – 25
00156222 P/V/G $24.99

33. PEANUTS™
00311227 P/V/G $14.95

34 CHARLIE BROWN CHRISTMAS
00311228 P/V/G $16.99

35. ELVIS PRESLEY HITS
00311230 P/V/G $14.95

36. ELVIS PRESLEY GREATS
00311231 P/V/G $14.95

44. FRANK SINATRA – POPULAR HITS
00311277 P/V/G $14.95

45. FRANK SINATRA – MOST REQUESTED SONGS
00311278 P/V/G $14.95

46. WICKED
00311317 P/V/G $16.99

49. HOLIDAY HITS
00311333 P/V/G $15.99

53. GREASE
00311450 P/V/G $14.95

56. THE 1950S
00311459 P/V/G $14.95

61. BILLY JOEL FAVORITES
00311464 P/V/G $14.95

62. BILLY JOEL HITS
00311465 P/V/G $14.99

63. MAROON 5
00316826 P/V/G $14.99

64. GOD BLESS AMERICA
00311489 P/V/G $14.95

65. CASTING CROWNS
00311494 P/V/G $14.99

68. LENNON & McCARTNEY FAVORITES
00311804 P/V/G $14.99

69. PIRATES OF THE CARIBBEAN
00311807 P/V/G $15.99